# A WEEK IN THE LIFE
# OF AN
# AIRLINE PILOT

# A
# WEEK IN THE LIFE
## OF AN
# AIRLINE PILOT

## WILLIAM JASPERSOHN

**LITTLE, BROWN AND COMPANY**

BOSTON TORONTO LONDON

## BOOKS BY WILLIAM JASPERSOHN

*Bat, Ball, Glove: The Making of Major League Baseball Gear*
*The Ballpark: One Day Behind the Scenes at a Major League Game*
*A Day in the Life of a Marine Biologist*
*A Day in the Life of a Television News Reporter*
*A Day in the Life of a Veterinarian*
*The Ghost Book*
*Grounded*, a novel
*How Life on Earth Began*
*How People First Lived*
*How the Forest Grew*
*How the Universe Began*
*Ice Cream*
*Magazine: Behind the Scenes at* Sports Illustrated
*Motorcycle: The Making of a Harley-Davidson*

The map on pages 6–7 was drawn by Martha Tusek, Country Graphics, Stowe, Vermont.

The cutaway drawing on pages 14–15 appears courtesy of the Boeing Aircraft Corporation, Everett, Washington.

The photographs on pages 57 (*bottom*), 59 (*bottom*), and 92 appear courtesy of Pan American World Airways, Inc., New York, New York.

Copyright © 1991 by William G. Jaspersohn

First Edition

Library of Congress Cataloging-in-Publication Data

Jaspersohn, William.
    A week in the life of an airline pilot / William Jaspersohn. 1st ed.
       p.    cm.
    Summary: Traces a pilot's journey to India in a 747 to provide
the reader a look at the duties and excitement of such a job.
    ISBN 0-316-45822-8
    1. Jet transports — Piloting — Vocational guidance —Juvenile
literature. [1. Air pilots. 2. Occupations.] I. Title.
TL710.J37   1990
629.132′5216′023 — dc20                 90-31792

10 9 8 7 6 5 4 3 2 1

MP

Published simultaneously in Canada
by Little, Brown & Company (Canada) Limited

Printed in the United States of America

*For Jim Marvin*

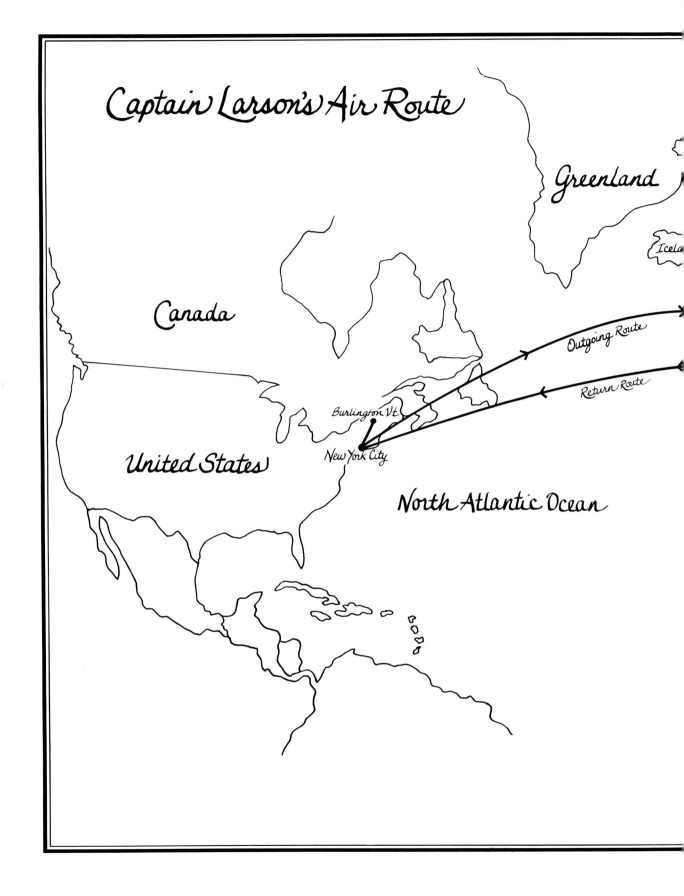

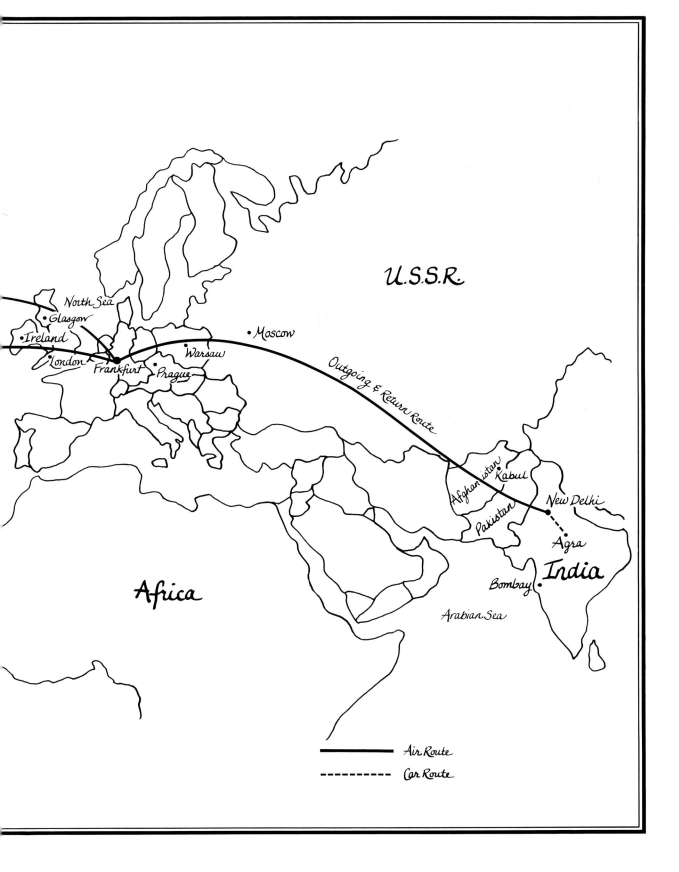

# FRIDAY

At noon on a cool day in late October, a man in the lobby of Vermont's Burlington International Airport eats a hot dog. He wears a blue-and-white-striped shirt and brown necktie. His tweed jacket is the color of post-autumnal Vermont hills. At his feet is a businessman's satchel. The hot dog is consumed in five businesslike bites. Several times a month for the past eighteen years, the man, airline pilot Captain Ralph Larson, has been commuting from this airport to New York, from where he flies planes internationally for Pan American World Airways. Since the planes he flies do not usually land in countries with menus featuring American hot dogs, eating one in Burlington has become a ritual for him. He likes them with mustard and onions, chased down with cups of coffee or sometimes an orange soda. Afterwards, pressing a fist below his sternum and ducking his chin, he will sometimes murmur, "Heigh ho, heigh ho," and then, bag in hand, he boards a plane that takes him to his calling.

During the plane ride to New York, Captain Larson performs another ritual: he removes his wristwatch and places it in his jacket pocket. As of tonight, the captain will fly through six time zones to Frankfurt, West Germany; and the day after tomorrow through another four and a half to New Delhi, India. After two days in Delhi, he will reverse tracks, returning through Frankfurt to New York. So daunting to him is the thought of passing back and forth through ten and a half time zones in seven days, that he will not use his watch during his entire week abroad. He says, "An old adage I learned as a Navy pilot goes, Eat when you're served, sleep when you're tired. I try to follow that adage when I fly. When an attendant brings me food during a flight, I eat it. When we're on the ground, if I'm tired, I sleep — doesn't matter if it's noon. As an airline pilot you can pass through so many time zones during a trip, that it's counterproductive to think about which time zone you've come from versus which you're in. A watch becomes irrelevant. So I put mine away."

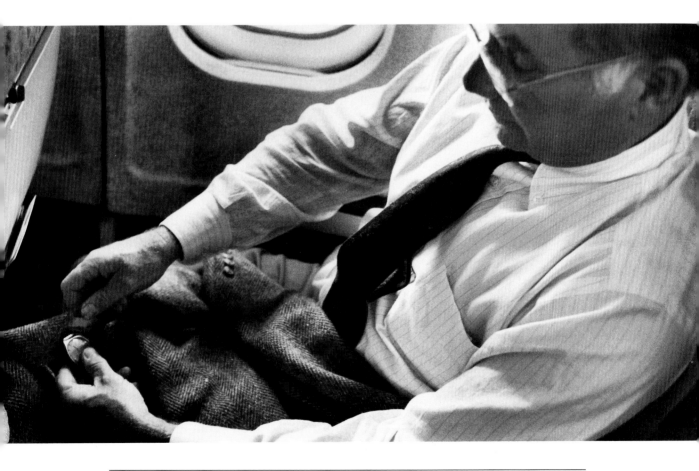

When he was a boy growing up on a seventy-two-acre farm out-side Chicago, Captain Larson dreamed of one day seeing the world. During World War II, he and his older brother, King, used to sit on the roof of the family hog barn and watch the trainees from nearby Glenview Naval Air Station go through their maneuvers in bi-wing Stearman airplanes. Of such viewings future careers are born. As swine grunted below him, Captain Larson envisioned himself in the sky, at the controls of such a plane. After deciding in his soph-omore year of college not to become a doctor, Captain Larson grad-uated with a degree in geology from the University of Illinois at Champaign-Urbana and enrolled in the Navy Aviation Officers Pro-gram at Pensacola, Florida. From 1960 to 1965, he flew A-4 Skyhawks — in California, Hawaii, and the Pacific, including Viet-nam. In 1965, with five years of Navy training under his belt ("the finest aviation training there is," he says), he was hired by Pan Am as a flight navigator. Over the years he has progressed from that post to flight engineer to first officer (copilot) to pilot. Today, he routinely flies passenger planes for Pan Am to Europe, Africa, Asia, and South America. His job has taken him nearly everywhere in the world, and yet, come vacation time, he will hop on a plane with his fam-ily — wife Janet, son Reeves, and daughter Susan — and jet to some

far-off locale. On their last vacation, a two-week trip in a dugout canoe on the Amazon River, the family fished for their food, swam in the brown river, and slept in native encampments. One day while fishing, the captain caught a piranha. The fish wriggled furiously on the hook, its face frozen in a piscine scowl. In all his life, the captain had never seen this species of man-eater before, and he suddenly realized how far from Illinois his life had taken him. He liked the realization. From his vantage on the roof of the hog born, the kid in him smiled.

On the twelve days or so a month when he is not flying for Pan Am, Captain Larson likes to split firewood from around his country home in Stowe, Vermont, or watch his own fish — rainbow trout — rise for chum to the surface of his pond. He wears his earned good fortune gracefully. In his worn jeans, flannel shirt, and heavy boots, he might easily pass for a logger.

The hour-long commuter flight from Burlington lands in New York, at La Guardia Airport, and from there Captain Larson takes a cab — or sometimes a shuttle bus — to John F. Kennedy International Airport, ten miles away. In all, the trip from Vermont to New York is relatively easy. By contrast, some Pan Am pilots live so far from New York that, to arrive on time for work, they must leave home the day before their piloting assignment and then sleep over in a hotel near the airport. Since that can get expensive, groups of pilots often rent apartments together near the airport and share the costs.

The first stop for Captain Larson at the Pan Am terminal is the pilots' room on the lower level. There, he goes to the operations desk to see which of the company's Boeing 747s he will be flying to Frankfurt tonight, and who his copilot and flight engineer will be. Like other Pan Am pilots, the captain "bids" a month in advance for the next month's flights he wants, and he never knows until the moment he checks in who his fellow crew members will be. Now he learns that his crew for the weeklong round-trip to New Delhi will include an old friend, First Officer Stan Cobb, from San Francisco, and a new man, Flight Engineer Bert Bertrand, from Tampa, Florida.

# BOEING 747

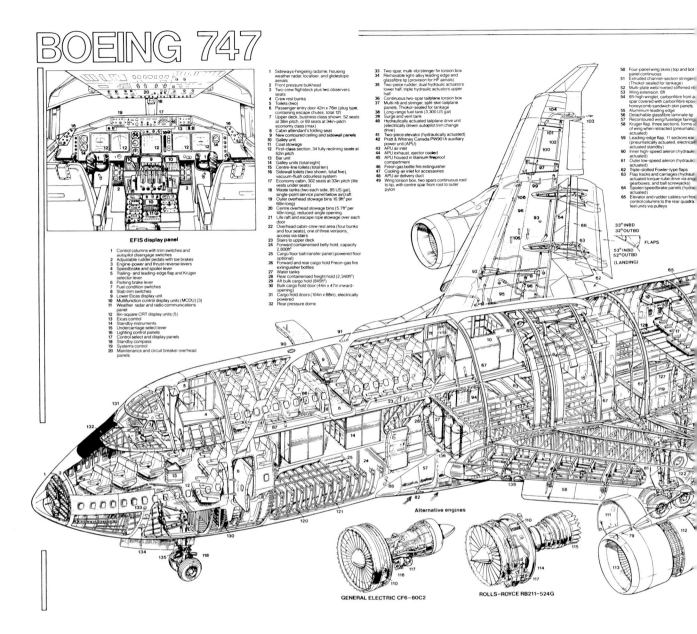

**EFIS display panel**

1  Control columns with trim switches and autopilot disengage switches
2  Adjustable rudder pedals with toe brakes
3  Engine-power and thrust-reverse levers
4  Speedbrake and spoiler lever
5  Trailing- and leading-edge flap and Krüger selector lever
6  Parking brake lever
7  Fuel condition switches
8  Stab trim switches
9  Lower Eicas display unit
10  Multifunction control display units (MCDU) (3)
11  Weather radar and radio communications panel
12  Bin-square CRT display units (5)
13  Eicas control
14  Standby instruments
15  Undercarriage select lever
16  Lighting control panels
17  Control select and display panels
18  Standby compass
19  Systems control
20  Maintenance and circuit breaker overhead panels

1  Sideways-hingeing radome, housing weather radar, localiser, and glideslope aerials
2  Front pressure bulkhead
3  Two-crew flightdeck plus two observers seats
4  Crew rest bunks
5  Toilets (two)
6  Passenger entry door 42in x 76in (plug type, containing escape chutes, total 12)
7  Upper deck, business class shown, 52 seats at 38in pitch, or 69 seats at 34in-pitch economy class (max)
8  Cabin attendant's folding seat
9  New contoured ceiling and sidewall panels
10  Galley unit
11  Coat stowage
12  First-class section, 34 fully reclining seats at 62in pitch
13  Bar unit
14  Galley units (total eight)
15  Centre-line toilets (total ten)
16  Sidewall toilets (two shown, total five), vacuum-flush odourless system
17  Economy cabin, 302 seats at 33in pitch (life vests under seats)
18  Waste tanks (two each side, 85 US gal), single-point service panel below aircraft
19  Outer overhead stowage bins 10.9ft³ per 60in long)
20  Centre overhead stowage bins (5.7ft³ per 40in long), reduced-angle opening
21  Life raft and escape rope stowage over each door
22  Overhead cabin-crew rest area (four bunks and four seats), one of three versions, access via stairs
23  Stairs to upper deck
24  Forward containerised belly hold, capacity 2,800ft³
25  Cargo floor ball transfer panel (powered floor section)
26  Forward and rear cargo hold Freon-gas fire extinguisher bottles
27  Water tanks
28  Rear containerised freight hold (2,340ft³)
29  Aft bulk cargo hold (845ft³)
30  Bulk cargo hold door (44in x 47in inward-opening)
31  Cargo hold doors (104in x 68in), electrically powered
32  Rear pressure dome
33  Two-spar, multi-rib/stringer fin torsion box
34  Removable light-alloy leading edge and glassfibre tip (provision for HF aerials)
35  Two-piece rudder, dual hydraulic actuators lower half, triple hydraulic actuators upper half
36  Continuous two-spar tailplane torsion box
37  Multi-rib and stringer, split-skin tailplane panels, Thiokol-sealed for tankage
38  Long-range fuel tank (3,300 US gal)
39  Surge and vent tank
40  Hydraulically actuated tailplane drive unit (electrically driven autopilot trim change drive)
41  Two-piece elevator (hydraulically actuated)
42  Pratt & Whitney Canada PW901A auxiliary power unit (APU)
43  APU air inlet
44  APU exhaust, ejector cooled
45  APU housed in titanium fireproof compartment
46  Freon gas bottle fire extinguisher
47  Cooling-air inlet for accessories
48  APU air delivery duct
49  Wing torsion box, two spars continuous root to tip, with centre spar from root to outer pylon

50  Four-panel wing skins (top and bottom) panel continuous
51  Extruded channel-section stringers (Thiokol-sealed for tankage)
52  Multi-plate web/riveted stiffened rib
53  Wing extension, 6ft
54  6ft-high winglet, carbonfibre front and rear spar covered with carbonfibre epoxy honeycomb sandwich skin panels
55  Aluminium leading edge
56  Detachable glassfibre laminate tip
57  Recontoured wing/fuselage fairing
58  Krüger flap, three sections, forms forward of wing when retracted (pneumatically actuated)
59  Leading-edge flap, 11 sections each (pneumatically actuated, electrically actuated standby)
60  Inner high-speed aileron (hydraulically actuated)
61  Outer low-speed aileron (hydraulically actuated)
62  Triple-slotted Fowler-type flaps
63  Flap tracks and carriages (hydraulically actuated torque-tube drive via angle gearboxes, and ball screwjacks)
64  Spoiler/speedbrake panels (hydraulically actuated)
65  Elevator and rudder cables run from control columns to the rear quadrant feel units via pulleys

33° INBD
32° OUTBD
FLAPS
53° INBD
52° OUTBD
(LANDING)

**Alternative engines**

GENERAL ELECTRIC CF6-80C2

ROLLS-ROYCE RB211-524G

The plane he will fly, a Boeing 747-100, is a long-range heavy transport fitted with seating for 412 passengers. Powered by four enormous turbofan jet engines, it is capable of a maximum speed in excess of 600 miles per hour; a maximum altitude of 45,000 feet; and a maximum range of 5,980 miles. The size of the plane is impressive — 231 feet 4 inches long, 63 feet 5 inches tall, and 195 feet 8 inches from wingtip to wingtip. So is its weight — 377,000

14

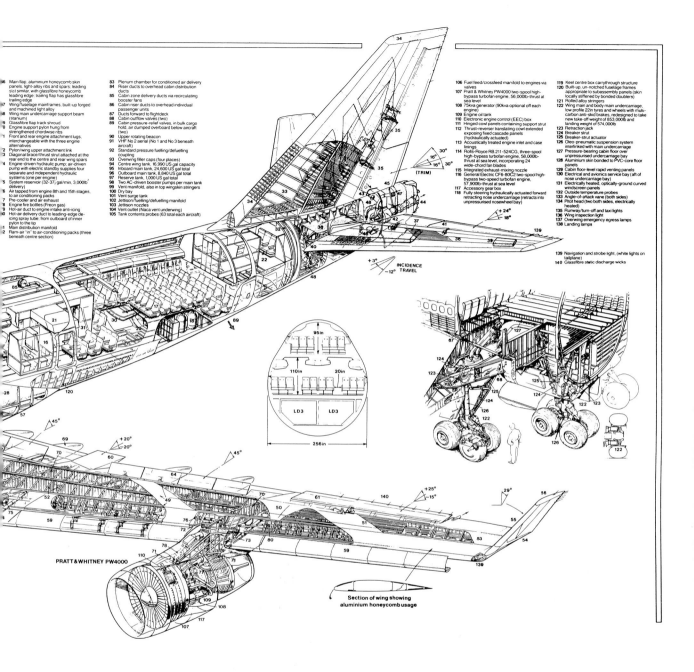

86 Main flap, aluminium honeycomb skin panels, light-alloy ribs and spars; leading slat similar, with glassfibre honeycomb leading edge; trailing flap has glassfibre trailing edge
87 Wing/fuselage mainframes, built-up forged and machined light alloy
88 Wing main undercarriage support beam (titanium)
79 Glassfibre flap track shroud
70 Engine support pylon hung from strengthened chordwise ribs
71 Front and rear engine attachment lugs, interchangeable with the three engine alternatives
72 Pylon/wing upper attachment link
73 Diagonal brace/thrust strut attached at the rear and to the centre and rear wing spars
74 Engine-driven hydraulic pump; air-driven pump with electric standby supplies four separate and independent hydraulic systems (one per engine)
75 System reservoir (32-37 gal/min, 3,000lb delivery)
76 Air tapped from engine 8th and 15th stages, to air conditioning packs
77 Pre-cooler and air exhaust
78 Engine fire bottles (Freon gas)
79 Hot-air duct to engine intake anti-icing
80 Hot-air delivery duct to leading-edge de-icing spray tube; from outboard of inner pylon to the tip
81 Main distribution manifold
82 Ram-air "in" to air-conditioning packs (three beneath centre section)

83 Plenum chamber for conditioned air delivery
84 Riser ducts to overhead cabin distribution ducts
85 Cabin zone delivery ducts via recirculating booster fans
86 Cabin riser ducts to overhead individual passenger units
87 Ducts forward to flightdeck
88 Cabin outflow valves (two)
89 Cabin pressure-relief valves, in bulk cargo hold, air dumped overboard below aircraft
90 Upper rotating beacon
91 VHF No 2 aerial (No 1 and No 3 beneath aircraft)
92 Standard pressure fuelling/defuelling coupling
93 Overwing filler caps (four places)
94 Centre wing tank, 16,990 US gal capacity
95 Inboard main tank, 24,600 US gal total
96 Outboard main tank, 8,840 US gal total
97 Reserve tank, 1,000 US gal total
98 Two AC-driven booster pumps per main tank
99 Vent manifold, also in top wingskin stringers
100 Dry bay
101 Vent surge tank
102 Jettison/fuelling/defuelling manifold
103 Jettison nozzles
104 Vent outlet (Naca vent underwing)
105 Tank contents probes (63 total each aircraft)

106 Fuel feed/crossfeed manifold to engines via valves
107 Pratt & Whitney PW4000 two-spool high-bypass turbofan engine, 56,000lb-thrust at sea level
108 75kva generator (90kva optional off each engine)
109 Engine oil tank
110 Electronic engine control (EEC) box
111 Hinged cowl panels containing support strut
112 Thrust-reverser translating cowl extended exposing fixed cascade panels (hydraulically actuated)
113 Acoustically treated engine inlet and case linings
114 Rolls-Royce RB.211-524CG, three-spool high-bypass turbofan engine, 58,000lb-thrust at sea level, incorporating 24 wide-chord fan blades
115 Integrated exhaust-mixing nozzle
116 General Electric CF6-80C2 two-spool high-bypass two-speed turbofan engine, 57,900lb-thrust at sea level
117 Accessory gear box
118 Fully steering hydraulically actuated forward retracting nose undercarriage (retracts into unpressurised nosewheel bay)

119 Keel centre box carrythrough structure
120 Built-up, un-notched fuselage frames appropriate to subassembly panels (skin locally stiffened by bonded doublers)
121 Rolled alloy stringers
122 Wing main and body main undercarriage, low profile 22in tyres and wheels with multi-carbon anti-skid brakes, redesigned to take new take-off weight of 853,000lb and landing weight of 574,000lb
123 Retraction jack
124 Breaker strut
125 Breaker-strut actuator
126 Oleo-pneumatic suspension system interlinked with main undercarriage
127 Pressure-bearing cabin floor over unpressurised undercarriage bay
128 Aluminium skin bonded to PVC-core floor panels
129 Cabin floor-level rapid venting panels
130 Electrical and avionics service bay (aft of nose undercarriage bay)
131 Electrically heated, optically-ground curved windscreen panels
132 Outside temperature probes
133 Angle-of-attack vane (both sides)
134 Pitot head (two both sides, electrically heated)
135 Runway/turn-off and taxi lights
136 Wing inspection light
137 Overwing emergency egress lamps
138 Landing lamps

139 Navigation and strobe light, (white lights on tailplane)
140 Glassfibre static discharge wicks

pounds when empty, though it is capable of carrying 428,000 pounds more.

Pan Am was the first airline to introduce the 747 to its passengers, in 1970. Since then, as passenger traffic has grown, the 747 has become one of the mainstays of the company's fleet, with thirty-five of them operating throughout the world.

Keeping a fleet in top working order is important, and Pan Am routinely schedules its planes for different maintenance procedures after they have flown specific numbers of hours. Just a week ago, in the maintenance hangar a few blocks from the Pan Am terminal at Kennedy, Captain Larson's plane went through a thousand-flight-hours maintenance check in which every system in the plane was serviced, and many parts, including a part of the landing gear, were replaced. Over a three-day period, twenty-five people worked on the plane for a total of two thousand man-hours, and only when all systems were approved was the plane allowed back in the air.

A similar schedule of careful maintenance is performed on the engines in Pan Am's aircraft fleet. The fanlike turbines in jet engines like these generate a great deal of power, called thrust, in order to push a plane through the air. In the process, however, heat is generated — some 1,500 degrees Fahrenheit of it. Over time, heat can wear an engine's parts down, so once a year, the back of each engine, called the hot section, with its system of turbines, is rebuilt; the worn parts are discarded and replaced. And every three years the entire engine goes through a complete inspection and overhaul. In between, no matter how well an engine is running, parts are replaced after they've flown a certain number of hours, and Pan Am ground crews at every company terminal throughout the world check the planes daily to be sure that all systems are running perfectly. "And even then," says Captain Larson, "the pilot and his flight crew also check the systems before, during, and after a flight. So things stay in top running order."

While the operations desk awaits further information about Captain Larson's plane, the captain himself, now changed into his navy blue uniform, fetches his mail in the crew mailroom. Then, because he will be flying all night and needs his rest (Eat when they feed you, sleep when you're tired), the captain naps for a few hours in the pilots' lounge.

At 6:00 P.M., when he awakens and returns to the operations desk for further information about his plane, he is greeted by a familiar voice that says, "Uh-oh, look who I got stuck with!"

The voice's owner is Stan Cobb, Captain Larson's copilot for the week, who's just flown in from San Francisco. A graduate of Annapolis Naval Academy and a former Navy test pilot, Stan is a twenty-year Pan Am veteran who's flown with Captain Larson many times. He warmly shakes the captain's hand. "How you doing, Ralph? It's nice to see you."

A minute later the two men are joined by Bert Bertrand, the flight engineer for the trip, who flew to New York from his home in Tampa earlier this afternoon. This trip to India is Bert's first — he's been with Pan Am for nine months and so far has flown only to Europe and the Caribbean. Prior to that he was a lieutenant colonel in the Air Force, stationed in Thailand, Vietnam, Arizona, California, Texas, and Italy.

"Good to have you with us," Captain Larson says, smiling. He shakes Bert's hand.

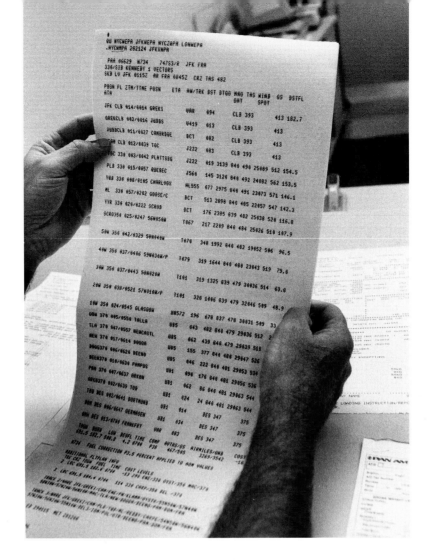

"Uh, Captain Larson?"

It is the operations clerk, ready with the paperwork for Pan Am Flight 66, the captain's flight to Germany. There is a loadsheet indicating the weight and balance of the aircraft. There is a flight plan outlining the route of the flight. A dispatch release that identifies the aircraft lists the length of the flight to Germany in hours and minutes, the fuel required for the trip, the aircraft's maximum take-off weight, and other important data. Captain Larson signs this release, indicating his agreement with it. A weather packet details weather conditions between New York and Germany for the next twenty-four hours. And a pretakeoff computation form, better known as a bug sheet, helps the captain compute the maximum speed at which he can stop the plane on the runway in case of an emergency.

Captain Larson and his crew carefully digest this information, which has been prepared for them by Pan Am's Dispatch office, in Building 208, where Aircraft Maintenance is also housed. Three hours before a flight, dispatchers feed data about the plane's weight and destination into a flight planning computer, which chooses a route for the plane that will ensure the most efficient fuel consumption. Dispatchers then check that route against weather conditions, schedule changes, slowdowns, and other factors, and if the computer's route needs modification, the dispatchers adjust it accordingly. In short, the Dispatch office takes care of all predeparture planning for a flight's crew, and even when a flight is under way, dispatchers can change a plane's route if necessary by radioing the pilot in the cockpit.

Working with Dispatch to help keep flights on schedule are the nearby Crew and Plane Tracking offices, which chart the whereabouts in the world of every one of Pan Am's 2500-plus pilots and 155 planes.

As the captain, Stan, and Bert read through their paperwork, passengers for Flight 66 are beginning to appear upstairs at the departure gate. Ticketing agents check the people's names against a computerized list and give them boarding passes, which, with their tickets, allow them to board the plane. Most passengers bought their tickets days, weeks, or even months ago through their own local travel agents or by phoning an 800 number for one of Pan Am's reservation sales centers.

The centers, located in Miami, New York, and Washington, D.C., are open twenty-four hours a day, three hundred sixty-five days a year, and each handles nearly a million calls a month. Many of the reservations clerks are bilingual, and calls can be handled in any of twenty-seven different languages. If one center's five hundred or so agents are busy, a call can be switched immediately to either of the other two centers, and on average a caller need wait only twenty seconds or less for a clerk to become available.

In return for their services, Pan Am's reservations clerks are paid an hourly wage plus benefits that include free travel for the agent and his or her family to any country in the world that Pan Am services. That benefit is available to all Pan Am employees, and it's not uncommon for even a baggage handler to knock off work in New York, say, on a Friday afternoon and hop on a Pan Am jumbo jet with his or her family for a long weekend in Paris. Or Rio. Or Nairobi, Kenya. As one company official puts it, "We encourage our employees to travel because it broadens their experience as individuals and makes them better appreciate what providing quality service means."

Captain Larson himself is planning a hunting trip to Mexico after his return from India. But for now, with his 747, Clipper Flight 66, fueled and waiting for him at the gate, and with its 369 passengers ready to board, their luggage secure in the plane's aluminum belly, it's time to put aside thoughts of vacation and go to work.

"Well, she looks good from here," says Stan, surveying the massive silver aircraft poised before them on the tarmac.

"That she does," says Captain Larson, and squaring his shoulders, he leads the march up the stairs and into the plane.

# SATURDAY

In the wee hours of Saturday morning, as most of the passengers sleep, Captain Larson and his crew guide Flight 66 to Europe. Since leaving Kennedy Airport in New York at 9:00 P.M., Flight 66 has followed a northeasterly course over New England and eastern Canada. Forty minutes into the flight, the captain announced to Stan Cobb, "We are now flying over my trout pond." Forty minutes after that, Flight 66 received radio clearance from a place called the Oceanic Control Tower in Gander Bay, Newfoundland, to continue its passage across the North Atlantic. Now the aircraft is two hundred miles south of Greenland, a small speck over a vast ocean. The wind blows steadily at an angle behind it: a quartering wind. At 33,000 feet — the plane's cruising altitude — the wind speed is eighty-seven knots: roughly one hundred miles per hour. A nearly full moon illuminates the aircraft's passage. With its panels of lighted instruments, the flight deck, where the captain and crew sit, resembles a glowing beehive.

As Flight 66 moves through the air, four invisible forces — weight, lift, thrust, and drag — act upon it to make it fly. Weight is the downward pull of gravity, which prevents the aircraft from shooting off into space and guarantees it will land on the earth again. Lift is what helps hold the airplane in the air. It occurs when the air pressure on the upper surface of the plane's wings is less than the air pressure on their lower surface. Creating lift requires thrust, which for the captain's plane is provided by its four jet engines. Because of the shape and angle of the plane's wings, and thanks to the engines' thrust, air moves faster and farther over the wings' upper surfaces than over the lower surfaces. Long ago, air scientists learned that the faster air moves along the top of a surface, the less air pressure on it and the more air pressure underneath it. On Captain Larson's plane, the greater air pressure underneath the wings pushes the airplane upward. The plane flies. A variety of movable flaps on the wings and tail help steer it. And the power of the jet engines overcomes a resistance called drag as the plane moves through the air.

Inside the flight deck, the captain controls the plane from his place in the gray seat to the left. The seat is electrically maneuverable up and down and backward and forward, densely padded, and extremely comfortable. In front of the captain is a device mounted on a thick rod and shaped like the letter **W**, called the yoke. It controls the flaps on the wings, called ailerons, which, when they move up or down, help steer the plane left or right. The yoke also controls the movable surfaces on the tail called the elevators; their movement up or down controls the up-and-down movement of the plane. At the captain's feet, meanwhile, are the rudder/brake pedals. By pushing with his feet on the bottom of the pedals, the captain can move the plane's tail rudder left or right, which also helps steer the plane from side to side. By pushing with his feet on the top of the pedals, he can apply the landing gear's brakes.

So that the first officer can fly the plane, his place on the right side of the flight deck has exactly the same controls and instruments as the captain's. On a console between the two seats are the throttles, which control the engines' thrust.

Bert Bertrand's job as flight engineer includes monitoring the gauges at his station that tell him how the aircraft's many systems are working, and operating switches that perform various functions. In New York, he turned on the plane's built-in generators that supply electricity to it. He turned on the heating and air-conditioning units so that the crew and passengers would be comfortable throughout the flight. He helped start the jet engines, flipped switches that control the fuel supply to them, and worked the throttles on the takeoff so that the captain and copilot would be free to steer the plane and talk to the control tower. As soon as a plane leaves the ground, the atmospheric pressure inside it begins to drop, and it if were to get too low, it could be harmful to everyone on board. So Bert switched on a device called a turbocompressor, and the plane's atmospheric pressure quickly stabilized to about that of Denver, Colorado. Also, when he called the departure gate for a pre-takeoff passenger count, he learned that the plane was carrying a dog in the aft cargo hold. Since the air temperature at 33,000 feet can be more than sixty-five degrees below zero, Bert switched on the aft temperature control to keep the dog at a cozy 70 degrees Fahrenheit.

The question many people ask Captain Larson about flying big planes across oceans or other wide spaces is, "How do you know where you're going?" The answer is, by means of two sophisticated pieces of equipment on board the aircraft, which work in conjunction with each other. The first is a combination computer-gyroscope called an inertial navigation system, or I.N.S.; the second is the autopilot, which can automatically fly the plane. Every day, according to wind patterns and other factors, flight planners for Pan Am, working with the oceanic control towers in Gander, Newfoundland, and Shannon, Ireland, divide the Atlantic into a variety of different flight routes called tracks. In New York, Captain Larson received his flight plan — the track he would take over the North Atlantic Ocean — broken down into a series of points along the line of travel called way points. Each way point is shown on the flight plan as a pair of numbers, called coordinates. The first, the latitudinal coordinate, indicates the plane's position compared to the equator; the second, the longitudinal coordinate, indicates the plane's position

along the length of the earth. Where the two coordinates meet (intersect) is the way point. Now, so that the plane follows the precise flight plan, the captain (or Stan) feeds the coordinates in order into the I.N.S. Then, using the altitude selection control, he dials in the altitude at which the plane should fly. Finally, once the plane has attained cruising altitude, he flips on the autopilot. A seeming miracle thereupon occurs. The I.N.S. gives signals to the autopilot, causing it to fly the plane from way point to way point. Straight and true, Flight 66 moves along its assigned track. "It's a neat system," the captain says admiringly, "the same one used on the space shuttle. In fact, the autopilot, nicknamed George, is so sophisticated we use it to land the aircraft when visibility is poor. Most of the time it does the job better than we could — *most* of the time. Frankly, we all feel that sometimes George can be a little rough."

As with most other systems on the plane, if one I.N.S. or auto-pilot fails, there are backup systems ready to take over. One of the captain's and Stan's jobs throughout the flight is to watch the I.N.S. to make sure both it and the autopilot are working properly. As the plane reaches a way point, its coordinates flash on the I.N.S.'s digital display. Captain Larson checks the coordinates against those on the flight plan and then radios the plane's position to one of the two oceanic aircraft control stations.

The radio's microphone is a thin tube attached to each crew member's headset. To send a voice message to a station, the captain turns a dial to the station's frequency, pushes a button on his steering yoke, and speaks. To receive a voice message, he takes his thumb off the button and listens through his headset.

Each oceanic control station is responsible for monitoring approximately half of the upper North Atlantic — Gander to the west, Shannon to the east. Since Flight 66 has now passed into Shannon's territory, Shannon now takes the captain's call, listening as he reports the plane's coordinates and giving him clearance to proceed on course for Frankfurt.

Dawn, and far below, heavy clouds shroud the Atlantic. The sun, a hard orange disc, peeks from behind white cotton tufts. The captain and crew are hungry. As if on cue, a flight attendant unlocks the cabin with her master key and asks if she can bring anyone food. The response is unanimous and affirmative.

Earlier in the flight the attendant served the crew dinner: salmon, rice, mushrooms, and salad. Along with the ten other attendants on board, she fed the 369 passengers. She loaded the plane's videocassette player for the evening movie. She brought the crew coffees and sodas. Now, from a small refrigerator in the upper-deck galley behind the flight deck, the attendant removes three prepackaged breakfasts — omelette, toast, and sweet rolls — and heats them for fifteen minutes in the galley's electric oven. The food, loaded in New York an hour before takeoff, was prepared near the airport by a private catering company.

Bert watches his gauges: the rate of fuel burn, oil quantity, oil temperature, oil pressure for each engine; reviews the plane's maintenance log; watches his gauges some more. The captain tells him his radar screen is malfunctioning. It's not a major problem — there are two other radar systems on the plane — but Bert will write up the malfunction in the Maintenance Log Book, and a Pan Am ground crew in Frankfurt will look into it.

In 1927, when a twenty-five-year-old pilot named Charles Lindbergh, alone in his silver single-engined plane, the *Spirit of St. Louis*, became the first person ever to fly nonstop across the Atlantic, he had no radar. He had no I.N.S., no autopilot, no radio. His flight suit featured a fur collar. He had no heater or air-conditioning. When he was hungry he ate a sandwich. When he wanted to see in front of him, he used a periscope. His flight plan included thirty-seven way points, and he guided the plane to them using only a compass, a sextant, and a chart of the North Atlantic that he spread across his lap. Six years later, with his wife, the writer Anne Morrow Lindbergh, he made survey flights for a fledgling airline company called Pan American Airways. From New York, the couple flew to Greenland, Iceland, Scandinavia, Russia, and Britain to plot a transatlantic passenger route, and when they returned to the United States, they answered a congratulatory message from President Franklin D. Roosevelt with this telegram:

THE PRESIDENT
THANK YOU VERY MUCH FOR YOUR MESSAGE STOP OUR TRIP HAS MADE US MORE CONFIDENT THAN EVER OF THE FEASIBILITY OF ESTABLISHING REGULAR TRANSATLANTIC AIRLINES IN THE NEAR FUTURE STOP ANNE LINDBERGH CHARLES LINDBERGH

The Lindberghs' voyage opened up the Atlantic for regular passenger service, and over the years the couple charted other routes for Pan Am. Charles Lindbergh himself went on to become a director of the company, and one of Captain Larson's biggest thrills as a young flight engineer was meeting Lindbergh on a flight to Hawaii.

"You met Lindbergh?" says Stan as he and the captain watch their gauges and await breakfast. The hero's name still stirs a feeling of reverence in airmen everywhere.

"What was he like?" Bert looks up from the Maintenance Log.

"He was outstanding," says the captain. "First-rate, you know? There's no overestimating his contribution to aviation."

"I smell smoke," Bert says.

The captain smells it, too. He scans the panel of electrical circuit breakers above his head, and seeing none tripped, quietly orders Bert to go back and investigate the passenger section. "It's probably nothing," the captain says. He checks the fuse panel again. A long minute passes before Bert returns, grinning.

"Sweet rolls burning in the downstairs oven," he reports. "False alarm."

In the *Spirit of St. Louis*, Lindbergh had one, or less than one, of every system he needed to cross the Atlantic; by contrast, Flight 66 has, on average, three of every system it needs. Or four. Or more. Had there been a real emergency, the crew would have shut down the offending system and, in most cases, would have been able to switch to a backup. And if they couldn't solve the problem themselves, they could call Pan Am's Airline Technical Control in New York, which would advise them on the proper solution. Lindbergh couldn't have called anybody; with no radio, he was absolutely alone.

On Flight 66, if either the captain or first officer leaves the flight deck for any reason, the person who is left alone must don his oxygen mask as a precaution against sudden emergency. "We work as a team now," says Captain Larson. "We avoid risks. We've come a long way from Lindbergh's day. Air travel's a heck of a lot safer."

At 4:00 A.M. New York time, land comes into view, and in a matter of minutes, Flight 66 is over Scotland, its hills pale heather and tweedy green in the morning light. "They've got a light frost down there," says Captain Larson. A short while later, the flight attendant enters the cabin. "Are you going to do wakeup now?" she asks the captain.

"Sure." He switches on the plane's intercom and delivers a brief message to the passengers, welcoming them to Europe, inviting them to look out their windows at Glasgow, six and a quarter miles below. "We should be arriving in Frankfurt at five-thirty New York time," he says. "That's eleven-thirty Frankfurt time." Then the autopilot angles the plane over the North Sea, and Captain Larson takes out his piloting charts of the Frankfurt area to refamiliarize himself with them.

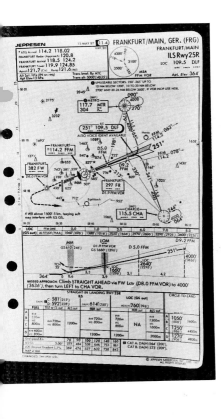

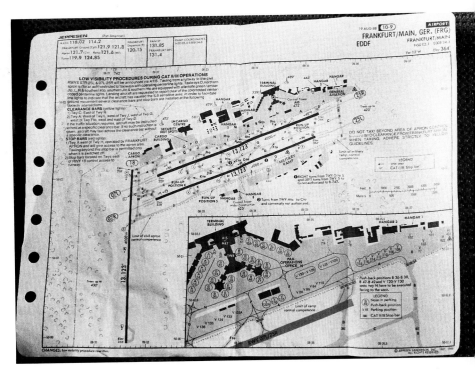

The first chart he studies shows the approach routes to Frankfurt Airport, and these, as they are for any airport, are well defined. They even show coordinates and altitudes for holding patterns — areas in the sky where planes can circle — in case air traffic is heavy and the control tower can't let Flight 66 land right away.

The second chart shows the layout of the airport itself, with its two active runways that are each 13,123 feet long. When Flight 66 gets within eight miles of the airport, the control tower there will tell the captain on which runway to land. Over the next hour, as Flight 66 moves closer to its destination, the captain and Stan radio their position to control towers along the route, and 105 miles from Frankfurt, the plane automatically begins its descent.

Twelve miles from Frankfurt, after the plane has automatically descended to ten thousand feet, Captain Larson turns off the autopilot and flies the plane himself. To continue the plane's descent into the Frankfurt area, he gently pushes the yoke forward, lowering the elevators on the plane's tail, and causing the plane's nose to drop. Then he pulls the yoke back somewhat to level off; after a moment, he gently pushes the yoke forward to descend more. He keeps doing this, pushing forward and pulling back, and the plane descends from ten thousand feet all the way to seven thousand feet in a matter of several minutes. The captain cuts the throttle significantly and the plane descends even more. Below, puffy cumulus clouds slightly obscure the green German countryside with its dark patchwork of tilled fields and oak-covered hills. The plane is within eight miles of Frankfurt. On the plane's radio, the Frankfurt control tower clears Flight 66 for immediate landing on Runway 25R. Minutes earlier, Bert had called out a predescent checklist. Now, at four thousand feet, he begins calling out an approach checklist to the captain:

"Altimeter."

"On, set, two-nine-two."

"Landing gear."

"Down — green light."

"Autobrake."

"Medium."

"Fasten Seat Belt sign."

"On."

"Exit sign lights."

"On."

The list continues through a dozen more items, and Frankfurt appears below. Once the site of an ancient Roman settlement, it is now a glittery trading capital, home to a variety of high-tech industries and many of West Germany's largest banks. "That's the Main," says Captain Larson, pointing to the river that bisects the city. The plane steadily descends. On the radio, over and over, a recorded voice says, "This is Frankfurt IMF, Runway 25, right. This is Frankfurt IMF, Runway 25, right . . ." Soon, in front of the plane is the runway, black and straight, and then there is the slightest bump and Captain Larson lands the plane. Flaps called spoilers, or speed brakes, automatically flip up from the upper wing sections, slowing the plane. Brakes inside the landing gear wheels slow it further. From the control tower, a ground-control supervisor directs the captain to steer the plane to Gate B46.

To steer the plane to the gate, the captain does not use the yoke, but rather a tiller located on the cabin wall to his left. The tiller turns the front landing gear wheels, allowing the captain to steer the plane on the ground in any direction.

As he nears the gate, he watches the hand signals of a Pan Am ground crewman, who guides Flight 66 along a set of painted lines. When the plane's front wheels touch a certain mark, the ground crewman crosses his arms over his head, and Captain Larson applies the landing gear brakes. A movable exit ramp is jockeyed into place. Flight 66 has arrived.

As soon as the plane stops, the captain makes sure the ground crew chocks the wheels with concrete blocks to prevent the plane from rolling, and then he and the crew shut the plane down. They switch off the I.N.S. systems, the fueling systems, the engines. They read out loud through an after-landing check to make sure that every system that's supposed to be off is off. They review their flight plan along with the I.N.S. readings to see how accurate the autopilot and I.N.S. were throughout the flight. Most of the time, the amount of error over an eight-hour, four-thousand-mile trip like this one is less than two miles, and today, there is no error whatever.

As the crew rises to disembark, a maintenance man enters the flight deck. Bert tells him about the radar problem and his write-up of it in the Maintenance Log.

"*Ja wohl*," says the maintenance man, seating himself at Bert's station. "We fix."

In his white cap and navy tunic, carrying his satchel and pilot's briefcase, Captain Larson leaves the plane via the crew gate. Like any foreigner entering a foreign country, he must pass through customs, where an official checks his passport and, in effect, approves his entry into West Germany.

Bert and Stan are already on the sidewalk outside the terminal when Captain Larson arrives, and now they all wait for the driver of the minibus that will take them to Frankfurt.

"Are you planning on doing anything today or tonight?" Stan asks the captain.

"I don't think so," the captain says. "If I hadn't seen it the last trip, I might go to the Frankfurt Zoo. Have you ever seen it? Yeah, it's great. But I'm tired, so I think I'll sleep this afternoon, get up, read the novel I brought, have dinner, and call it a night. What about you guys?"

"I'm going to a Halloween party tonight, believe it or not," Stan says. "Some German friends invited me, and it ought to be fun."

"I'm probably going to read and watch television," says Bert. Everyone agrees a man hasn't lived if he hasn't seen the TV show *The Munsters* dubbed in German.

By noon, checked into their hotel, the Intercontinental, their rooms booked and paid for by Pan Am, the crew sleeps. Their schedule allows them a full day of rest, and they take advantage of it.

At six o'clock, after an afternoon siesta, they reconvene in the hotel lobby and walk two blocks to the Basler Eck Restaurant for dinner. Although it is a public eatery, the Basler Eck, better known to Pan Am flight crews as the Gas Station, has become, over the years, a kind of unofficial private club for flight crews passing through Frankfurt. Captain Larson calls it "a place where you meet, eat, relax, gossip, joke, and see friends you haven't seen in years. Don't ask me why — maybe it's another one of my rituals — but when I'm there, I always have schweinhockze [pork hock], red cabbage and home fries *mit* onions. It's a place that fits like a comfortable pair of shoes, and after a seven-hour flight, you want that."

# SUNDAY

At 9:00 A.M. Sunday morning, the crew is back at Frankfurt Airport, refreshed after a good night's sleep and ready to fly to New Delhi, India.

On his way to the plane, Captain Larson stops by an operations desk just like the one in New York to pick up his flight's paperwork, and then he visits with four of the eleven attendants who will be working on the plane today. The attendants are all from India; they routinely work flights from New Delhi or Bombay, where they live, to Frankfurt and other European cities. "How will the weather be over Eastern Europe and Russia today, Captain?" one of them asks brightly.

She isn't just asking for asking's sake. Passengers will want to know today's flying conditions, and a bumpy flight can make an attendant's work more difficult.

"Overcast," says Captain Larson. "Eastern Europe tends to get socked in with clouds this time of year. The charts show that we may see a little air turbulence, but it shouldn't be too bad."

While the captain and Stan board the plane, Bert Bertrand goes outside on the tarmac to perform his visual inspection of it. Visual inspections are a regular part of a flight engineer's job, and Bert performs his briskly but carefully. He walks beneath every inch of the plane, noting especially the condition of the engines and the landing gear, and the degree of wear and tear on the tires.

As he makes his walk, a fuel truck loads the tanks located in the wings with a total of 253,000 pounds of jet fuel. Although the flight to India is only 4,400 miles, the truck crew pumps in enough for the plane to travel nearly 1,000 miles farther if flight conditions require it.

On the other side of the plane, one of the cargo hatches is open to receive a load of cargo containers filled with passengers' luggage. Cargo containers make handling the luggage a lot easier, and the containers fit comfortably in the plane's holds.

As for food, today's flight will include lunch and dinner, and these individual prepackaged meals are loaded from an elevated van into the plane's refrigerators in the galley on the main level.

Inside the plane, a private cleaning crew is hard at work, vacuuming the aisles, filling the overhead bins with fresh lap robes and pillows, dusting the seats, and wiping the armrests. And a security agent who works at the airport performs his own special safety check.

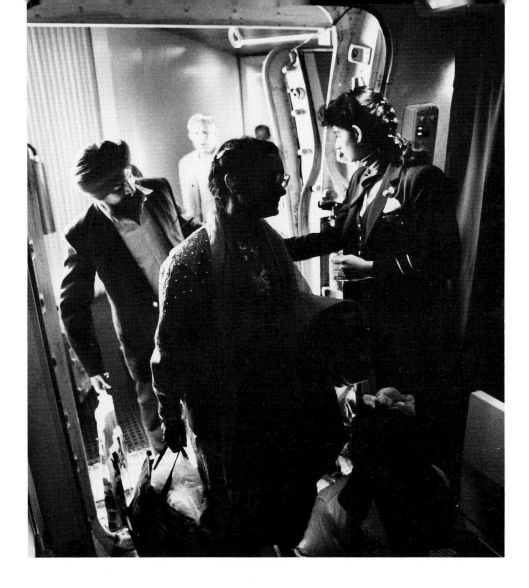

Soon, as in New York, the plane's gate opens and passengers laden with belongings appear in the doorway. "Good morning," says the flight attendant. "Welcome to Flight 67 to Delhi." Many of the four-hundred-plus passengers today are Indians returning home after a period of business or pleasure in Europe, and their clothes reflect their Indian culture. Some of the men wear turbans and light cotton trousers, and the women, colorful ankle-length silk dresses called *saris.* Though most speak English, some address the flight attendants in Hindi, the principal language of India.

"*Namaste,*" says a bearded man. ("Hello.")

"*Namaste,*" replies the attendant. "*Aap kaise hein.*" ("How are you?")

"*Bahut acha. Dhanyavad.*" ("Very good. Thank you.")

On the flight deck, the atmosphere is much like that of a study hall, with everyone carefully doing homework. In New York, Captain Larson had announced that Stan Cobb would fly the plane from Frankfurt to Delhi so that "I can talk to the Russians," and now both Stan and the captain review departure routes from Frankfurt, using their charts and the flight plan prepared for them by the Frankfurt Dispatch office. They discuss the amount of fuel they are carrying, and Captain Larson says, "That's not enough. We need more," and radios the ground crew to add another 22,000 pounds.

When the fuel is in the tanks, the captain begins calling out the prestart checklist, and then the start checklist. When he calls "Turn number one!" Bert reaches up to the ceiling panel and flips a thick switch that activates an air-driven starter motor. The turbines in engine number one begin to whine. Captain Larson watches a gauge that indicates the turbines' r.p.m. (revolutions per minute). When they reach 22 percent of their maximum, the captain flips a fuel lever on his control panel to the Start position, sending fuel and electricity to the engine. The engine fires. Bert and the captain repeat the procedure for the three other engines, Flight 67 receives clearance from the control tower to leave its gate, and a ground crewman, driving a heavy-duty diesel tug, backs the plane from the terminal.

In order to have enough lift to take off, Flight 67 must attain a certain ground speed based on its weight, which, today, is 749,000 pounds — "about as heavy as you can get," Bert says. Based on this weight, today's takeoff speed, known as V2, is 171 miles per hour; it was determined earlier by Stan and the captain, who looked it up on graphs in their flight manuals. Along with V2, Stan and the captain also determined Flight 67's V1 — the maximum runway speed at which it will still be safe to stop the plane in case of an emergency, and its VR, the speed at which the plane's nose will lift off the ground. Based on the aircraft's weight, these speeds are 161 and 167 miles per hour, respectively.

When Flight 67 taxis out to the end of the runway and receives permission from the control tower to take off, Stan, piloting the plane, lifts his feet off the brakes, pushes the throttles forward, and, using the rudder pedals, steers the plane straight down the runway's center stripe. The plane accelerates smoothly. Bert keeps his hands on the throttles to steady them, and Stan watches the aircraft's ground speed. All systems remain Go. The plane passes V1. It reaches VR. With the end of the runway almost near, Stan pulls back on the yoke a predetermined number of degrees, and Flight 67 is airborne.

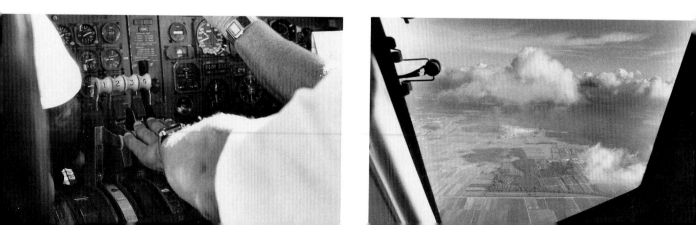

As Stan flies the plane, one of the many instruments he scans is the attitude indicator, which serves as an artificial horizon for him and shows him when the plane is level. When Captain Larson was first learning to fly in the Navy, he would go up in a trainer plane with his flight instructor seated behind him and practice what Stan is doing now: keeping the plane level. The flight instructor carried a joystick, and if the plane happened to dip, Captain Larson would feel a sharp jolt on the back of his helmet and hear the instructor's voice through his earphones, shouting, "Larson!" *Thwack!* "Keep your nose up!" *Thwack!* "Keep your nose up, Larson! You hear me?" *Thwack!* "In that way," says the captain, "I learned how to use the attitude indicator."

But flying a 747 is not like riding a bicycle where once you know how to do it, you always can. It takes continual practice to know how to cope with the different situations that can occur during flight — especially during takeoffs and landings. To keep its flight crews prepared for any situation, Pan Am requires them to report twice a year to the Pan Am International Flight Academy in Miami for refresher training in the academy's flight simulators. Captain Larson usually makes the four-day visit in January, when the weather in Florida is pleasant, and he always stops by to chat with Captain Roy Butler, the head of the academy and an experienced pilot.

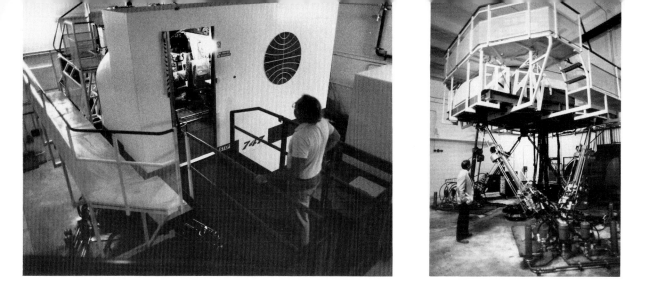

Because there are always so many pilots taking refreshers at the academy, sessions on the simulator start early, around five o'clock in the morning. Captain Larson always arrives in Miami the day before so he can be sure to have a good night's sleep before the training session. When the session starts, he enters the simulator from a platform behind it, and once he is inside with a copilot, flight engineer, and two instructors, the door to the simulator is locked and the platform moved away.

Inside, the simulator looks just like the flight deck of a real 747. Computer-operated hydraulic lifts can cause it to move in various directions, simulating the sensation of real flight, and video monitors on the windscreen project images of nighttime runways and cities that change in position as the aircraft "moves." By pressing buttons that lead to the computer, the instructors can present the flight crew with an array of different problems, including engine fires, landing-gear malfunctions, and sudden losses of power on takeoff. "We can load in a combination of problems," says an instructor, "and correct pilots the moment they make the wrong move. The idea is to drill them to make the right move by reflex, so that in a real situation they'll do it automatically."

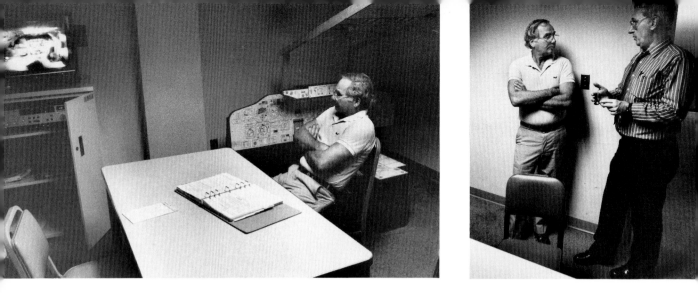

After two hours in the flight simulator, Captain Larson goes to an adjacent room and views his videotaped performance. He also talks each situation through with the chief instructor, listening carefully to his suggestions and discussing other solutions to particular problems.

Then, on a cardboard simulator, the captain prepares for a session that will test his understanding of the 747's controls. Cardboard simulators are a standard training device used by the military since World War II. "They don't look like much," says Captain Larson, "but they're a useful way to practice control sequencing, again, so it becomes automatic."

The rest of a refresher course is spent in the classroom, reviewing plane systems and emergency procedures. Captain Larson says, "There's always something new to learn — you can never know enough about flying — which is one of the reasons I like my job. You can never sit back and say you know it all."

Besides its flight crews, Pan Am also trains its flight attendants at the academy. New trainees undergo six-week training in everything from meal preparation to emergency procedures, and veteran attendants return once a year for refresher training. Three of the most anticipated exercises for both new and veteran attendants include wearing a self-contained oxygen hood and fighting a fire on board a plane mockup, sliding down a 747's emergency exit slide, and practicing water evacuation procedures by jumping fully clothed into a swimming pool and setting up an emergency life raft. "Is my job fun?" an attendant says. "Yes, I suppose it is. Even jumping into the swimming pool. Long flights can be tiring, but visiting foreign countries makes the occasional hard flight bearable. I love to travel, and with this job I can truly say I'm seeing the world."

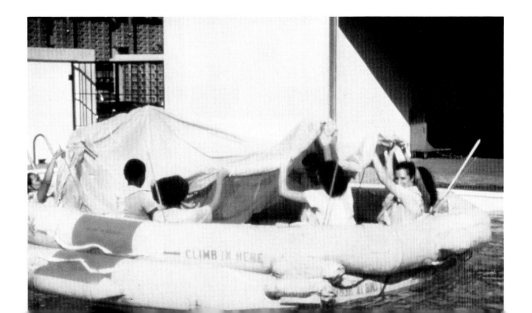

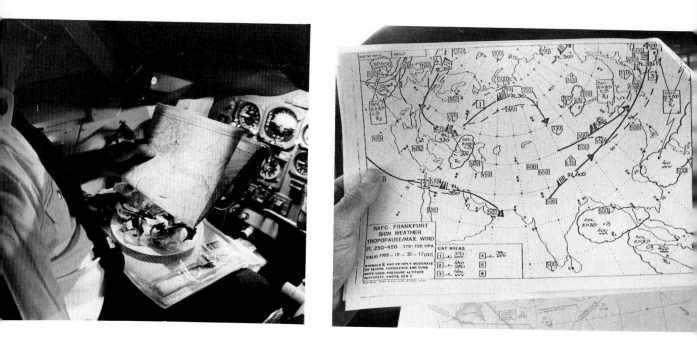

Back on Flight 67, Captain Larson studies the weather charts and eats a simple Indian vegetarian meal: spiced potatoes, carrots, beans, and cauliflower with *chappatis* (thin flour pancakes) and, for dessert, curried pineapple with coconut. Since the plane follows the earth's eastward rotation, dusk comes early. The sky behind the plane turns orange and pink.

Earlier, as the captain had predicted, cloud cover increased from Berlin to Warsaw, although not before the crew glimpsed snow on the dark earth of eastern Poland and ice on the gray rivers flowing into Russia. Now, over Belyy, a small city 150 miles west of Moscow, the captain informs Stan of the possibility of C.A.T. (clear air turbulence) ahead, and Stan switches on the Fasten Seat Belt sign, indicating to passengers that they should remain in their seats with their seat belts fastened. "It probably won't be heavy," says the captain. "But better to be on the safe side."

Captain Larson also talks to the air traffic control centers en route, radioing the plane's position at each way point. On flights over other parts of the world, way points come at intervals of twenty to forty-five minutes. Over the Soviet Union, they come roughly every five minutes. "The Russians like to know where we are," says the captain, "and sometimes they can be difficult, repeatedly asking for more information. But today they're being super pleasant, which, I can tell you, is a relief."

On Bert's table an alarm clock sounds. He switches it off and consults a gauge on his panel. In a log he writes down the total amount of fuel used so far by each engine: about 54,000 pounds. There are 232,030 pounds left. Each engine, Bert calculates, is burning fuel at a rate of about 1.7 pounds per second. "That's not too bad," he says. Later, maintenance people in New York will feed Bert's information into a computer to study how efficiently the engines are running. He resets the alarm for twenty minutes. He looks at the fuel thermometer. When the temperature drops below 45 degrees Fahrenheit, he switches on the aircraft's fuel-heating system. This makes sense. The air temperature outside the plane is a brisk minus-65 degrees Fahrenheit. Fuel at that temperature will jell — freeze — and not be able to pass through the fuel lines. So Bert heats it. His supper arrives: venison, wild rice, and carrots. He eats, watching his gauges. He activates new tanks of fuel as they're needed. And he makes sure the fuel stays warm.

Into the quickening night, Flight 67 continues. The I.N.S. is programmed for New Delhi, India. The plane flies smoothly at 600 miles per hour. The crew stays busy: the captain calculating the plane's E.T.A. (estimated time of arrival) to each way point, Bert watching his gauges, Stan loading more way points into the I.N.S.

Over Afghanistan, Stan says, "Look, that's Kabul, the capital, out there, about fifty miles away." He dims the flight deck's lights. Kabul, in the darkness, looks like a sparkling mat. A few miles away from it, five orange dots of light suddenly appear, forming an arc over the darkened ground. They burn brighter, illuminating the terrain: mountains. They are Russian parachute flares, Stan says. The Russians are fighting the Afghanis.* The flares are fired to reveal the positions of U.S.-made Stinger missiles and the missiles' guardians, the Afghan freedom fighters. The fighting between the two countries has been going on for almost nine years. The flares' brightness lends a reality to the conflict that no TV news report or newspaper headline can match. Yet Flight 67 is safe passing Kabul, its identity known by the Afghani control towers, its route recognized by the Russians and Afghanis alike. Stan says, "I dropped a lot of parachute flares doing reconnaissance flights in the Navy."

Had he always wanted to be a pilot? someone asks. "No," he says. "In New Middletown, Ohio, where I grew up, my dad ran a creamery. All through my childhood, I helped him make ice cream and cottage cheese and butter, and it was just naturally assumed that when he retired I'd take over. But somewhere along the way I got into Boat School [the U.S. Naval Academy at Annapolis], and after I graduated, I started flying airplanes. Why did I start flying? I guess because I thought it was exciting, taking off on aircraft carriers and all that. I guess the Navy liked me, because after my four years' sea duty, they made me a test pilot. In fact, I was one of one hundred semifinalists chosen for the Apollo astronaut program, but I didn't make finalist — I think because I hadn't been a test pilot long enough. That was in 1964. In 1967, I retired from the Navy and went to work for Pan Am, at first as a technical manager, and later as a pilot. It's a good life. My wife, Helga, flies for Pan Am, too, as a flight attendant, and, you won't believe this, I taught my son Rick to fly and now he's a flight engineer for Pan Am and stationed in Berlin. At age twenty-two. In a year or so he'll have his first-officer

*Not anymore. — Author

qualifications and be the youngest pilot in the company. Isn't that outstanding?"

Over the Khyber Pass, between Afghanistan and Pakistan, the crew begins to prepare for landing. Stan studies the charts of Delhi's Indira Gandhi Airport. Bert tests the landing lights located on the wings. Captain Larson radios the plane's position to an Indian ground station near Lunkaransar, in the Great Indian Desert. Throughout a journey, professionalism reigns on the flight deck, intensifying most, it seems, during takeoffs and landings. With clarity and care, Bert answers Stan's questions about electricity, oil, and fuel. Smoothly and precisely, the captain dials in a lower altitude on the altitude selection control. He inserts it into the I.N.S. computer by pushing the Insert button on the panel. The throttles automatically drop a hair from their cruising position, and the plane begins to descend.

Over New Delhi, whose lights spread as infinitely as those of Los Angeles, each man adjusts his chair up and forward, electrically, for the final descent. The plane is off autopilot now, and Stan steers with the yoke. He smoothly works the throttle. The attitude indicator shows that the plane is level, and the altimeter near it reads 6000 feet and dropping. Stan releases a lever that lowers the landing gear. Twin orange vertical lines — the runway — appear ahead. Bert begins calling out the descent checkoff list. The plane's headlights go on. The plane goes down gently. It touches with a slight bump. Clipper 67 is on the ground. At the moment of touchdown, Stan hits the brakes. A rabbit runs out on the runway, the first sign of Indian wildlife. As the captain and crew later discover, it will not be their last.

It is 12:30 A.M. New Delhi time, but somewhere around Atlantic Ocean time according to the flight crew's body clocks. The journey has been nine hours long. Everyone now feels glassy-eyed and a little tired. Stan yawns. The captain sighs. Bert's eyes move around, taking in the new surroundings. In the airport, passengers are queued at the customs windows, and the wait to clear customs could be a long one.

Captain Larson stops an airport official. "Excuse me," he says, showing his company identification badge. "We're the flight crew from Pan Am Flight 67 from Frankfurt and — "

"Oh, yes, Captain, of course, of course. Gentlemen — " The official speaks with a crisp English accent. "Come right this way, sirs. Yesyesyes, this way, please. Very good."

He ushers the men through a separate customs window for pilots, and in a few minutes the captain and crew find themselves walking into the warm New Delhi night.

It is noisy outside the terminal. Big trucks lumber along the access road to the terminal, buses roar, horns honk. And then there is the smell. In his essay on the famed Anglo-Indian writer Rudyard Kipling, the poet T. S. Eliot wrote: ". . . the first condition of understanding a foreign country is to smell it." India's odor is a rich combination of many perfumes: dust blown eastward from the Great Indian Desert, vehicle exhaust, animal dung, charcoal smoke, cooking spices, incense, flowers, body sweat, mildew, and human excrement. For many Westerners visiting India for the first time, this stew of pungencies is shocking. No guidebooks or photographs of the country have adequately prepared them for it. They can't quite believe their own noses. They instantly feel foreign, even to themselves. "You never get used to it," says the captain. "I've been flying to India for fifteen years, okay? And it's always a surprise."

A man with a rifle awaits the crew on the sidewalk. He is their security guard. Several months ago a flight crew for another airline was attacked by an armed man as they boarded their crew bus. No one was hurt, and the attacker was arrested, but since the incident Pan Am has required that its crews change out of their uniforms before leaving planes, and they've posted a guard on each crew bus to ensure their crews' safety. Other airlines have taken similar precautions. And the Delhi police have beefed up airport security. "It's a pain in the neck to change out of your uniform, especially when you've had a long flight," says the captain. "But I appreciate the company's concern for us, and it makes sense to be careful."

At the Maurya Sheraton in New Delhi, the captain and crew check in. Stan says he has to turn his watch ahead four hours from Frankfurt time, and one of the desk clerks corrects him. "You mean, four and a *half* hours." India is one of a number of countries in the

world — Saudi Arabia and Newfoundland are others — with an irregular time zone of ninety minutes rather than an hour.

After a late-night snack of toasted cheese sandwiches with hot Indian peppers and beer, the flight crew begins to wind down. Bert and Stan make plans to go shopping at noon in downtown New Delhi, but the captain begs off, saying he wants to make plans for a car trip on Tuesday to Agra, 150 miles to the south. "Besides," he says, "I always buy something from those street vendors, and nine times out of ten, when I get home, I wonder why I bought it, and it winds up in the hall closet. So you go ahead without me. See you tomorrow night for supper."

# = Monday =

The avenue in front of the hotel is hot and bustling with traffic when Bert and Stan take a cab at noon to downtown New Delhi. Although India gained its independence from a century of British rule in 1947, it has retained certain British peculiarities, among them the left-hand flow of traffic on its thoroughfares. From their Ambassador cab, driven by a young man named Ram, Stan and Bert see swarms of cars, trucks, motorcycles, motor scooters, bicycles, pushcarts, and rickshaws. People in loose-fitting clothes walk the sidewalks. Stan says India's population is 800,000,000 and growing by a million people a month. Bert wonders aloud if the birth rate will ever slow down. Stan says, "I don't think so." Earlier, they had been warned not to visit the historic Red Fort in nearby Old Delhi today because 2,000,000 people would be there to commemorate the death of former Prime Minister Indira Gandhi, who was killed by an assassin in 1984. Another 2,000,000 Indians — farmers — are at a place called the Boat House, not far from the flight crew's hotel, to protest what they feel is the imbalance of wealth between the cities and rural areas. The shopping district, says Stan, will not be so crowded.

Stan is right. At the first place they visit, a government-sponsored crafts shop called Cottage Industries, there are few other customers and the clerks lavish their attention on Bert and Stan. They show them marble boxes inlaid with fifteen varieties of semiprecious stones. No sale. They dangle bead-encrusted purses on gold chains, inviting the men to touch the delicate needlework. Stan says, "I just don't know if Helga would want something like that." Two clerks unroll no fewer than fifty Oriental rugs, until Stan says, "I'll be coming back next month," and Bert says, "I'll bet you said that last month." The clerks shrug. They usher the men to a back room. They ply them with warm Campa Colas. Sapphires lie in the mountains of Kashmir in northern India, and the clerks have sackfuls of sapphires. They have cut them into domes and ovals, and as a result, the sapphires display the six-pointed star pattern for which they are named. Bert buys a lavender star-sapphire necklace for his wife, Sandy, haggling the clerk's price of 1350 rupees (about $90) down to 1150 rupees (about $80). Bert's negotiation does not offend the clerk. In India, purchasing anything without a haggle is inconceivable.

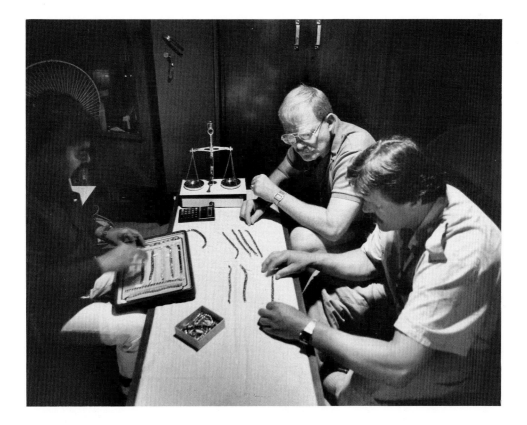

Outside the shop, the men are assailed by vendors. One tries to sell them a brass lock in the shape of a lion, another proffers a scented, hand-carved chess set. ("It smells. You smell it. See? Smells.") Others wave postcards, embroidery needles, bracelets. But the most enterprising street merchants, by far, are two teenage boys who shout, "Snake? Snake? Snake?" and from a burlap bag one pulls a six-foot-long python, while the other lifts the lid off a low circular basket, and up pops a four-foot black cobra. The boy prods the cobra with a stick, produces a tiny mongoose on a leash from under his sleeve, and begins playing a squawking tattoo on a bulbous flute. The moment it is touched, the cobra flares its hood. The mongoose darts from side to side on its leash. The snake is confused. The python holder drapes the snake around his neck. The cobra darts and turns.

The flutist beckons Stan nearer.

"Maybe you wish to play for snake, sir?"

"No way! That thing's liable to strike my bare leg!"

"Then maybe the mongoose on your neck?"

"Uggh!"

"Or python?"

"Get me outta here!"

"I sell you everything — snakes, flute, mongoose. One thousand rupees!"

"No!"

"All right. Eight hundred!"

"Where's Ram?"

"Six hundred!"

The men climb into their taxi.

"Five hundred rupees, flute and cobra!" The boy shoves the basket toward the cab window.

"What's the matter," Bert says to Stan as they ride back to the hotel, "you afraid of a little snake?"

That night before supper, Bert and Stan tell the story of their adventure to Captain Larson and a friend of Stan's, Anil Kaul, a resident of New Delhi and a pilot for Air India.

"I will let you in on a little secret," says Anil when he hears about the snakes. "Those cobras are defanged. The boys buy them from snake merchants. They are no more snake charmers than you or I."

"There, you see?" says Bert to Stan, his eyes smiling with amusement. "That snake wouldn't hurt you."

"Yeah? Then why, when they appeared, did you stay one step behind me?"

"Age before beauty," Bert replies, and everyone laughs.

# TUESDAY

For his car trip to Agra the next morning, Captain Larson rises early. He eats an omelette and toast in one of the hotel's restaurants, and at 5:00 A.M. stands with the doorman, waiting in the predawn mist for the car to arrive.

The doorman is a Sikh. The Sikh religion is one of eight major religions in India — the others are Hinduism, Jainism, Buddhism, Islam, Zoroastrianism, Christianity, and Judaism — and its followers believe in one god and the virtues of piety and strength. Unlike Hindus, Sikhs condone killing animals for food and reject the Hindu belief in nonviolence. In person, they appear fierce and warriorlike, and yet Captain Larson finds them friendly and always helpful to him as a foreigner.

"So where do you go this morning, sir?" the doorman asks, smiling.

The captain tells him his destination.

"Ah, then you will be having a full and absorbing day," says the doorman. And with that he straightens and snaps a salute as the car arrives.

The driver, Mr. Oswal, smiles at Captain Larson, revealing teeth stained red from chewing betel nuts. Betel nuts, the seeds of the betel palm, are a sharp-tasting, mildly addictive stimulant chewed by many Asians for the same reasons that other people smoke cigarettes. Mr. Oswal keeps a small supply in his shirt pocket.

He opens the car door for the captain. "To Agra, right?" the captain says. Mr. Oswal says nothing, but flashes his red smile and nods.

Outside Delhi, the road is congested. Vehicles of all descriptions generate dust. Besides cars and trucks, Captain Larson sees bullock carts, camel carts, mule carts, elephant carts, motor scooters, bicycles, and rickshaws. Whole families sit in motorized rickshaws, their belongings piled high around them. Farmers drive tractors loaded with jute and sugarcane. Huge trucks made by a company

called Tata carry freshly picked cotton to be spun into cloth. And everywhere there are cows. To Hindus, they are sacred, and they are protected from slaughter by government law. Several times, Mr. Oswal slams on the brakes to allow a cow to shamble across the road. Captain Larson smiles. Cows have been politely shooed out of Delhi, he says, but abound throughout the rest of India. Most have no owners and wander where they choose, and though Hindus gain religious merit feeding them, many cows along the road to Agra this morning look undernourished.

When Mr. Oswal stops at a tin-roofed stand in the village of Rosi to buy himself more betel nuts, a boy with a monkey appears at the car window. He holds up the monkey for the captain's inspection. He holds out his hand. The captain looks at the boy. The monkey looks sad and pensive. The captain gives the boy five rupees. The boy nods and smiles. Another car appears, this one with English tourists. The boy runs to it. The scene is repeated. In silence, the boy takes another rupee.

"India is full of extremes," the captain murmurs, and the scenes on the road to Agra bear him out. Near a billboard advertising a luxury hotel, children shape dung into bricks for fuel, and a stooped woman wielding a crude besom laboriously sweeps dust from the roadside. Within yards of expensive concrete houses, squatters' settlements teem with indigent families. Most of the settlements are without toilet facilities and running water, which explains the people relieving themselves in the brown fields, and also explains the women with earthenware jugs on their heads, walking to water wells miles away.

Mr. Oswal seems unperturbed by these disquieting scenes. Signs on truck tailgates read Honk Before Passing, and Mr. Oswal obediently honks. He leans on the horn, pressing it eight to ten times for every vehicle he passes. The noise is shattering. The captain mutters, "He's got to be the honking champ of all India." At that moment, as if in response, Mr. Oswal burps, downshifts the car to second gear, and speeds, honking, past an overturned bus.

In this way, Mr. Oswal brings Captain Larson to Agra by late morning. Once the capital of India, when Moghul conquerors from the north occupied the country, Agra today is a five-thousand-year-old city whose chief industry is tourism. Captain Larson visited Agra twenty-six years ago when he was a Navy pilot on leave from his aircraft carrier in the Indian Ocean. Today he is back to see Agra's chief attraction, perhaps the most famous building in all the world, the Taj Mahal.

The tour begins with Mr. Oswal stopping by a travel office in a shabby mall and picking up Captain Larson's guide for the day, Mr. Sethi. Mr. Sethi has a pleasant smile and speaks impeccable English. "Welcome to Agra, Captain." Mr. Sethi shakes the captain's hand. "Let us drive to the Taj and begin our tour at its Red Gate."

The entrance through the giant red sandstone gate is thronging with tourists when the captain and Mr. Sethi arrive. Written on the gate in Sanskrit lettering are words from the Islamic bible known as the Koran. Because of the way they have been proportioned, the letters in the words appear to be of uniform size, from top to bottom. "An optical illusion, you might say," says Mr. Sethi. "Shall we go in?"

Inside the gate, after buying his ticket, Captain Larson has his first view of the Taj in twenty-six years. He is hushed by the sight of the white domed building. Mr. Sethi is respectfully silent. The Taj seems to float above its long, narrow reflecting pool, a dreamlike apparition in the blue, shimmering heat. "Notice the minarets," says Mr. Sethi, pointing to the four pencillike towers at each corner of the temple. "They have been constructed at an angle away from the Taj, so that if they ever fall, the Taj itself will not be damaged."

"As you perhaps know," Mr. Sethi continues, "the Taj Mahal was constructed by the emperor Shah Jahan as a tomb for his wife, Arjumand, who died tragically in 1631, after giving birth to the couple's fourteenth child. Arjumand was known as *"Mumtaz Mahal"* — Jewel of the Palace. Her loss saddened Shah Jahan immeasurably. From 1631 to 1653, with the aid of architects and builders from all over Europe and the Middle East, he built what you see. Twenty-two tons of white marble inlaid with semiprecious stones make up the main edifice. Twenty thousand workers labored for twenty-two years to complete it. Then the gardens were laid out, and the two red sandstone mosques on either side were built, along with the gate and surrounding walls. Come, we will walk to the Taj and into the tomb itself."

Captain Larson sees a bullock-powered lawnmower on one of the side lawns and thinks, "I could use one of those in Vermont."

When visitors wish to enter the Taj Mahal, they must first remove their shoes, out of respect for the dead within. Captain Larson and Mr. Sethi leave their shoes near the Taj's front railing, and Mr. Sethi hires a man to stand guard over them.

"No photos," says a guard to a photographer in the crowd of tourists.

Mr. Sethi first leads Captain Larson up to the cenotaph, or empty tomb, under the monument's bulbous dome. It is dark and cool inside the cenotaph. Mr. Sethi switches on a flashlight. He waves it at the handcarved marble screen that surrounds the two marble dummy coffins. He presses its lighted head against the cenotaph's marble walls to illuminate the colorful inlaid stone work. "Isn't it beautiful," Mr. Sethi purrs, stroking it. "I never tire of visiting this room."

The real tomb, where the bodies of the Shah Jahan and his wife lie in coffins, is a dark, windowless chamber in the basement. The heat in the tomb is stifling. Indians press around Captain Larson, more curious about him than about the coffins' inhabitants. "*Chelo!*" Mr. Sethi shouts in Hindi. "Go away!" He shoos the crowd aside. Captain Larson feels as if he is suffocating in the tomb. "I'm ready to go upstairs," he tells the guide.

Later, the captain walks all around the Taj by himself, and then joins Mr. Sethi near the entrance gate to watch the people flow past. He would like to stay and sightsee more — perhaps visit the Agra Fort built by Shah Jahan from 1565 to 1573, or ride an elephant at one of the hotels near the Taj. But it's getting late, and the captain and crew must fly their 747 out of New Delhi tonight. The captain buys a necklace for his daughter, Susan, from a street vendor outside the Taj. Then, after paying Mr. Sethi his guide's fee and thanking him for his excellent services, he returns to the car and says to Mr. Oswal, "To Delhi."

Late in the afternoon, there is one more sight which, to Captain Larson, says as much about India as anything else he has seen. Rounding a bend in the road from Agra, the car comes upon a flock of vultures devouring the carcass of a bullock. In Bombay, India, 700 miles to the southwest, the captain has seen the Towers of Silence, the seven circular walled enclosures on the Malabar Hill where a religious group called the Parsis leave their dead to be eaten by vultures. "The Parsis do that," says Captain Larson, "because they believe it's wrong to pollute the three sacred elements, earth, fire, and water. The vultures pick the body clean, and afterward, the bones are thrown into a pit, where sand and charcoal filter the rainwater so that the disintegrating bones don't pollute the earth.

"Do I think all that's weird? No, to me it's just India. Thanks to

my job and all the places it's taken me, I've learned firsthand that other parts of the world can be very, very different from the United States. In our country there are people who'd drive through a flock of vultures like this one and try to kill them. But not here in India. Here, people respect the vultures and let them do their work. They accept them. They accept that whole cycle of birth, life, death, and rebirth, and maybe we Westerners can learn something from that acceptance."

The captain returns to the car.

"India opens my eyes," he says. "I don't always like what I see. But I learn something every time I come here, and the learning, the rubbing up against different cultures and countries — that, to me, is one of the best parts of being an airline pilot."

# WEDNESDAY/
# THURSDAY

No voyage is complete without a return, and Captain Larson's return to the United States after two and a half days in India is unexceptional. The night flight out of New Delhi goes without a hitch, despite the plane's takeoff weight of 723,000 pounds. The stars are bright, the sky as black as obsidian. Over India, Pakistan, Afghanistan, Russia, Poland, and Czechoslovakia, Flight 67 retraces the route it took three days earlier. The captain, Stan, and Bert are quiet and businesslike. The plane whooshes through the air, guided by its sophisticated nagivational equipment. In nine hours, the plane is back over Germany, and at 8:00 A.M. Frankfurt time, it makes its landing.

Twenty-four hours after that, the crew is back in the air, having rested once again at the Frankfurt Intercontinental Hotel and dined on Wiener schnitzel and fried potatoes at the Gas Station with other flight crews.

By one o'clock, Thursday, eastern standard time, Flight 67 spots land — Cape Cod, Massachusetts, its familiar elbow shape delicately edged in hazy sunlight. Rather than approach New York from the northerly route it took to Europe, the flight will approach from the east, over Long Island Sound. In the course of a week, the captain and crew have traveled eighteen thousand miles. Now, two hundred miles from Kennedy Airport, they begin preparations for their final descent.

The control tower at Kennedy Airport is ready for them. Typically, planes bound for Europe leave Kennedy in the morning and evening, while planes returning from Europe arrive in the afternoon. Most 747s returning from the north or east are instructed by the control tower to land on Runway 13 Right, or 13 Romeo, as it's called. It's 14,572 feet, or nearly three miles long — long enough to land a jumbo jet like Captain Larson's.

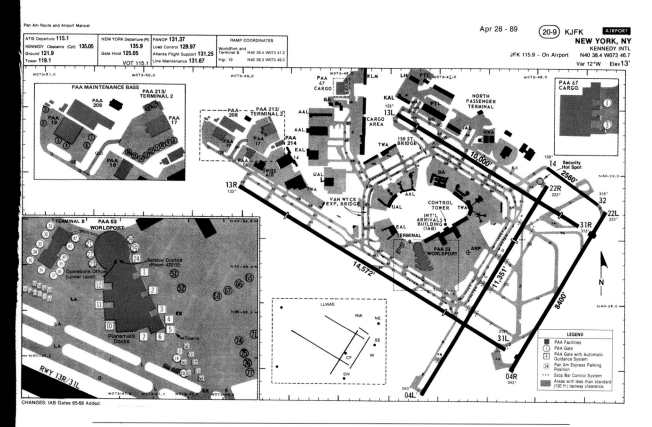

Shifts of seven air traffic controllers man the tower at all times. Each controller has a separate duty, and each rotates from duty to duty every one and a half to two hours.

At a center at MacArthur Airport on Long Island, a computer keeps track of every commercial airplane flying into or out of Kennedy Airport. The control tower at Kennedy receives the information for each flight on a strip of computer paper, and the strips of paper are put in order according to each plane's scheduled arrival or departure.

Once a plane is within eight miles of the airport, it is picked up on the tower's radar scopes, and a controller radios the plane's captain or copilot what coordinates to fly to next and when and on which runway they can land. It's a tricky job, but the controllers are highly skilled, and their efforts are well coordinated. On an average day, they can land planes at a rate of sixty an hour — one every minute — and at peak times that volume can reach eighty an hour — one every forty-five seconds.

Captain Larson has hand-flown Pan Am Flight 67 the last twenty or so miles, and the control tower gives him permission to land on 13 Romeo immediately. What is it like piloting a huge 747 compared, say, to piloting a fighter plane? "Piloting a seven forty-seven is like driving a big, comfortable, powerful truck," says Captain Larson, "while piloting a fighter jet is like driving a sports car. Each, in its own way, is fun to pilot, but you certainly sense the weight and size of the seven forty-seven behind you when you handle the yoke."

At 1:45 P.M., right on schedule, Flight 67 touches down.

"If you've got a minute, I'd just like to say, you made this trip," Captain Larson tells Stan and Bert when the plane is stopped at the terminal. In the captain's voice is a touch of emotion, which he quickly covers. "I mean," he says humorously, "could you imagine a double dose of something else?"

Everyone laughs.

"It's a pleasure, Captain," Bert says quietly.

"Thank you for having us," Stan says.

The crew does its checklists. It shuts down the plane. Bert writes up a minor malfunction in the Maintenance Log, and Stan climbs out of his seat.

"You flying back to San Francisco tonight?" the captain asks Stan, and Stan replies that he is. "How 'bout you, Bert?"

"I take the Tampa-St. Pete at five o'clock," he answers.

"Well, see you guys," says the captain, shaking both men's hands. "Let's do it again sometime."

When Charles Lindbergh returned to the United States after his historic transatlantic solo flight, he was greeted as a hero. He dined at the White House with President Calvin Coolidge, received the Congressional Medal of Honor, rode in a tickertape parade in Manhattan, and signed commercial contracts worth hundreds of thousands of dollars. By dint of being the first person to fly from New York to Paris, he had become, to many, the most famous young man in the world.

Because of Lindbergh's achievement, and the improvements in aircraft technology since his flight, Captain Larson finds himself returning, not to a hero's welcome, but to a cold pickup truck in an airport parking lot and to a long drive through sluggish traffic to Stowe. The captain doesn't mind. Flying has become routine now. "It's better that way." And yet, he says, there remains something exciting about taking a big plane up and cruising through the stratosphere and visiting someplace foreign. To the question of whether he likes his job, his answer is always an emphatic "Yup."

Now at home, nine thousand miles from New Delhi and the Taj Mahal, he is confronted by a simpler question. His wife, Janet, wonders what he wants for dinner. He has been waiting for this one since a week ago, when he left Burlington Airport. He says, "I'll just have a hot dog."

# ACKNOWLEDGMENTS

This book could not have been written without the special help and interest of Jeff Kriendler, Pan Am's vice president of corporate communications. Jeff is the consummate visualizer, and one of the most professional men I have ever met. I owe him an enormous debt of gratitude, not merely for his support for this project, but also for his trust in me and in my idea.

That debt of thanks extends to Jeff's support network, particularly Chickie Dioguardi and Susan Timper, and the late James Arey, who was the first to hear about and encourage me on the project, and who steered me to Jeff.

Rusty Bell, Pan Am's flight control manager in New York, was my guide through flight control operations and the control tower at JFK International Airport; my great good thanks to him and his staff for their hospitality and help.

My special thanks for their time and help also go to Captain Roy Butler and Captain Britt Williams at Pan Am's International Flight Academy in Miami; Charles Kennedy and his staff at Pan Am's reservations sales in Miami; Bruce MacConnie, John Reardon, and their staffs at Aircraft and Shop Maintenance in New York; Edward Trudeau, Duayne J. Orner, and the air traffic controllers in the JFK Tower; Anil Kaul in New Delhi, India; and Pat Kelly somewhere over the Atlantic Ocean.

My thanks, too, for their kindness, professionalism, and courtesy to every other Pan Am employee I encountered in the course of my research for this book — especially the flight attendants on all my flights both here and abroad, the airline technical control and flight tracking people in New York, and the ground crews in New York, Frankfurt, and New Delhi.

Finally, I wish to thank Captain Ralph Larson and his family for agreeing to be the subjects of my book; and Captain Stan Cobb and First Officer Bert Bertrand for letting me into their very special world. I shall always cherish memories of Bert and Stan haggling with a rug vendor on my behalf in New Delhi, and Ralph gets my vote as a world-class act. Thanks, guys.